Second World War (1939–1945)

0	1000 AD	2000 AD

300–146BC)

Anglo-Saxons (450–1066)

Tudors (1485–1603)

Victorians (1837–1901)

Romans (700BC–476AD)

Vikings (800–1066/1400)

Contents

Look up the **bold** words in the glossary on page 32 of this book.

Akhenaten

Thutmose III | Horemheb

1000 BC	0

Hatshepsut is first woman pharaoh

Ramesses II
Tutankhamun

Egypt is conquered by the Greeks

Time of the New Kingdom

Meet the ancient Egyptians

Here is a procession in ancient Egypt. The pharaoh is being carried on his throne by slaves. His wife, the queen of Egypt, is being carried behind him. In front of him are three members of his court.

There are some ordinary citizens of Egypt in the picture, too. A man and two women are on the right, and two boys are running alongside the procession.

Did you know… ?

- The word pharaoh is used to describe the king of Egypt.

- The ancient Egyptians actually called the pharaoh the 'Lord of the two lands' or the 'High priest of every temple'.

- When a pharaoh was crowned king the Egyptians believed that he was a living form of the god called Horus.

- Most people in Egypt were farmers.

Q Can you describe the pharaoh's crown?

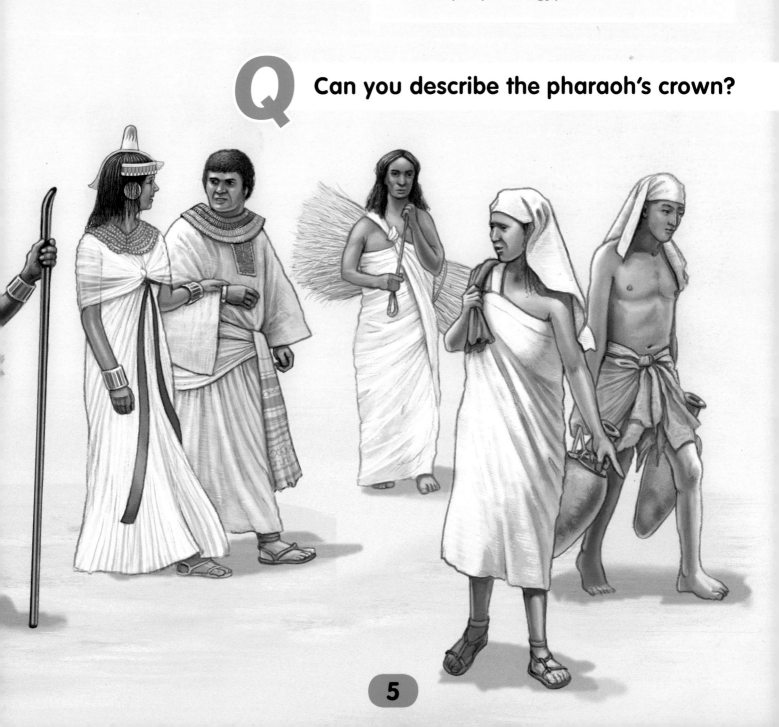

The Nile

When we visit Egypt, we find it is a desert land where the sun shines almost every day, where temperatures soar above 40°C in summer, and where it almost never rains. It would be impossible to live here if it were not for the River Nile, which runs straight through the desert and floods the land on each side every year.

The ancient Egyptians used the Nile water to drink and to **irrigate** their crops. They used it for transport too, and built many boats to sail on it.

As Egypt was rich and fertile, other people wanted to conquer the country, and were prepared to fight the Egyptians for it. This meant that the Egyptians had to have a strong army to defeat them.

As the Nile was so important to the ancient Egyptians, nearly all of their cities were built beside it. As a result, ancient Egypt was a long, narrow country, as you can see on the map.

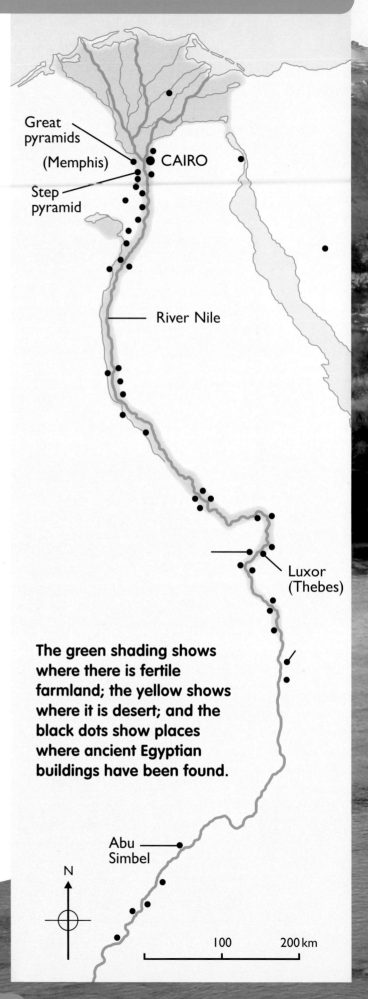

Great pyramids (Memphis)

Step pyramid

CAIRO

River Nile

Luxor (Thebes)

The green shading shows where there is fertile farmland; the yellow shows where it is desert; and the black dots show places where ancient Egyptian buildings have been found.

Abu Simbel

N

100   200 km

This picture shows the Nile near the city of Aswan. The river makes the land in the valley lush and fertile. The hills nearby are barren desert.

Did you know... ?

- The Nile is 6,700 km long. It is the longest river in the world.

- The Nile runs right through Egypt.

- The Nile floods land close to its banks once each year.

- The yearly river flood keeps the land in the valley fertile.

Q Why was the Nile so important in the lives of the ancient Egyptians?

Farming the black soil

As we travel down the Nile today, we see the black soil beside the river, and the farmers using oxen to plough it. The ancient Egyptians farmed the land in a similar way, but how do we know?

If we look at pictures of farming in the tombs of ancient Egypt, we also see farmers using simple ploughs behind pairs of oxen.

Look at the pictures of modern dates growing on a date palm (date tree) and then find more palms on the tomb painting.

This is a date palm grove. The brown fruits are dates.

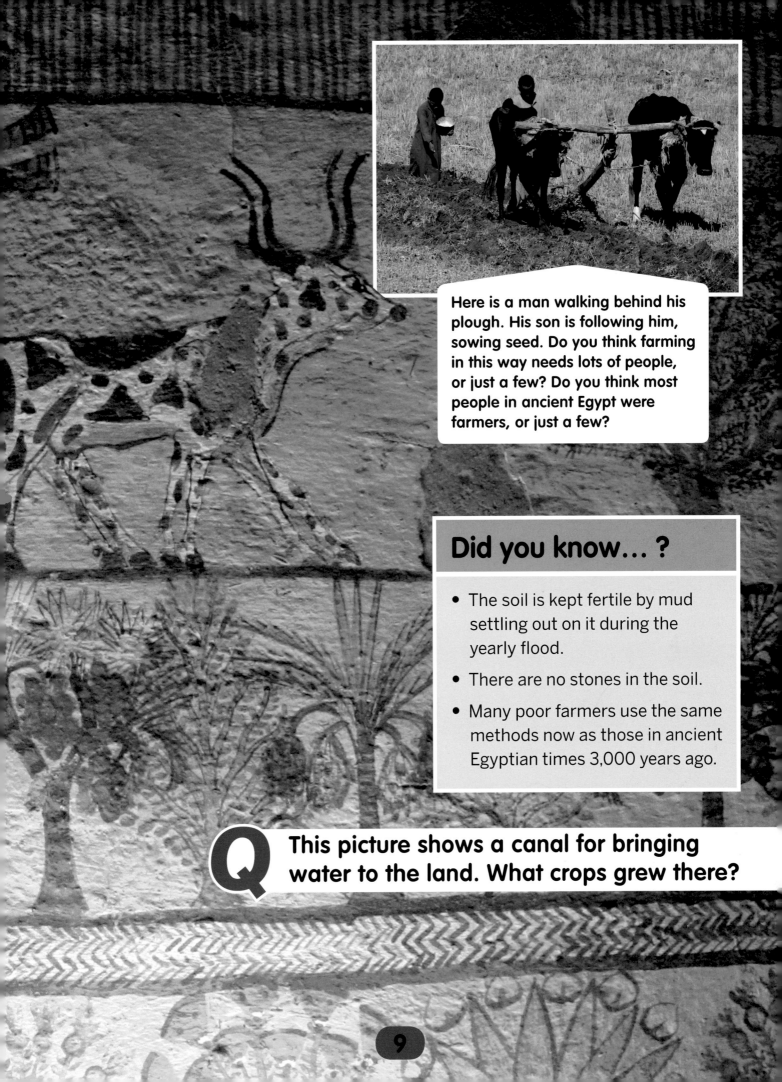

Here is a man walking behind his plough. His son is following him, sowing seed. Do you think farming in this way needs lots of people, or just a few? Do you think most people in ancient Egypt were farmers, or just a few?

Did you know… ?

- The soil is kept fertile by mud settling out on it during the yearly flood.

- There are no stones in the soil.

- Many poor farmers use the same methods now as those in ancient Egyptian times 3,000 years ago.

Q This picture shows a canal for bringing water to the land. What crops grew there?

Messages in pictures

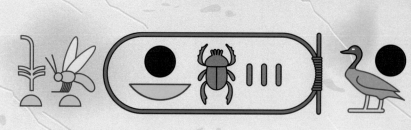

On every building that we see there are carvings of tiny pictures in rows and columns. This is how the ancient Egyptians wrote, using a picture to mean a letter or a word.

The pictures are called **hieroglyphs**.

They give many clues to how the ancient Egyptians lived, and the things that they believed in.

A cartouche is an oval which was drawn to contain the hieroglyphs that spelt out a king or queen's name. It's a kind of royal seal or signature. It was made up of two parts; the first name followed by the last name. Cartouches give important clues to the pharaohs who built temples and other monuments. This is the cartouche of Tutankhamun.

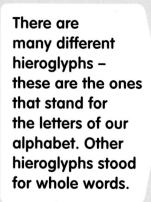

There are many different hieroglyphs – these are the ones that stand for the letters of our alphabet. Other hieroglyphs stood for whole words.

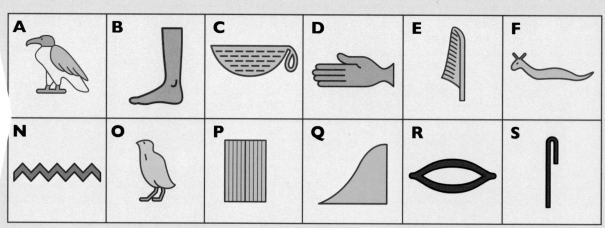

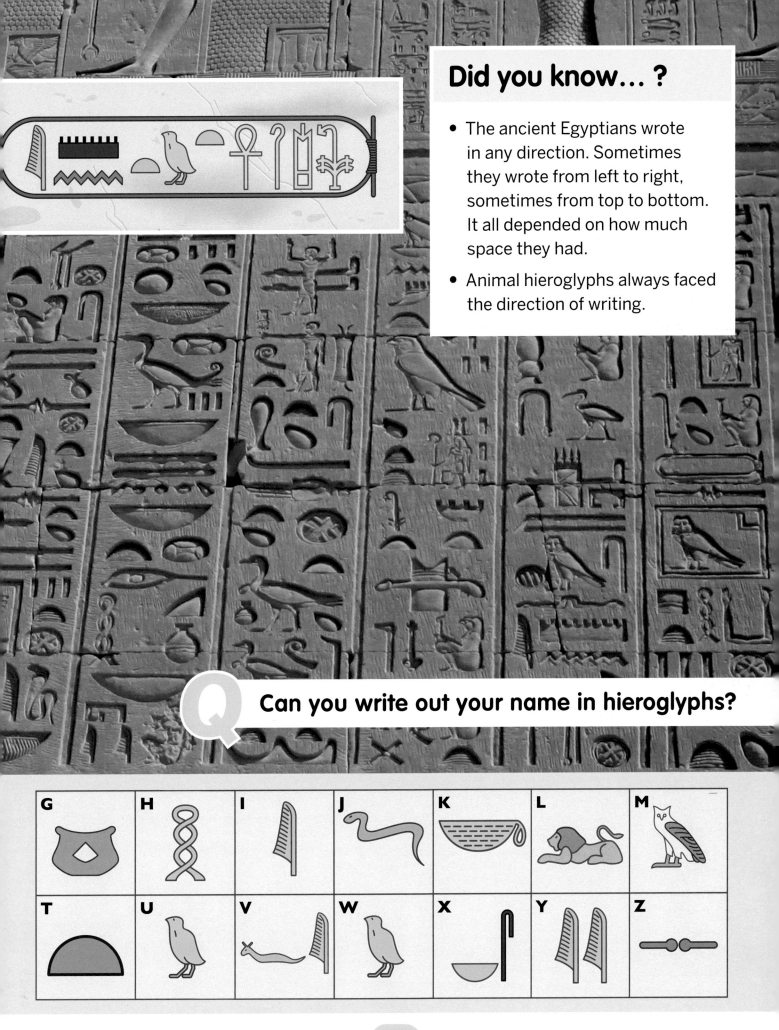

Did you know… ?

- The ancient Egyptians wrote in any direction. Sometimes they wrote from left to right, sometimes from top to bottom. It all depended on how much space they had.

- Animal hieroglyphs always faced the direction of writing.

Q Can you write out your name in hieroglyphs?

G	H	I	J	K	L	M

T	U	V	W	X	Y	Z

The pyramid builders

When we travel to Cairo, we see the skyline crowned by the three Great Pyramids. These pyramids are among the world's largest man-made things. They were built 4,500 years ago when this was the site of Memphis, which was the capital of the Old Kingdom.

There are over 100 pyramids in Egypt, but the three at Giza, next to Cairo, are very much bigger and better known than all the others.

All of the pyramids were once covered in polished white limestone and would have gleamed in the desert sunshine.

The three Great Pyramids were built in little under a century. After that, no more were built because it was too expensive.

This is the pyramid of Khafre – 136 m high with a base 210 m long. Some of the limestone blocks which once covered the whole pyramid still remain near the top. The rest have been taken away and used for other buildings.

This is the pyramid of Menkaure. It is 65 m high and has a base 108 m long. It was the third, and last of the Great Pyramids to be built.

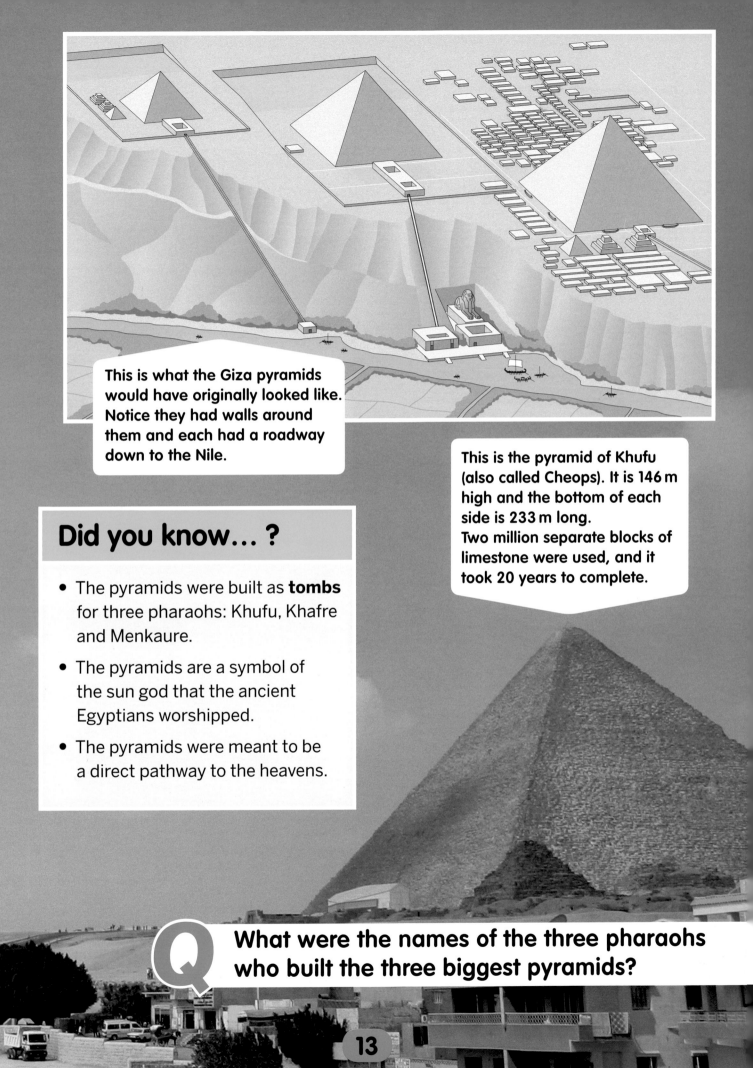

This is what the Giza pyramids would have originally looked like. Notice they had walls around them and each had a roadway down to the Nile.

This is the pyramid of Khufu (also called Cheops). It is 146 m high and the bottom of each side is 233 m long.
Two million separate blocks of limestone were used, and it took 20 years to complete.

Did you know… ?

- The pyramids were built as **tombs** for three pharaohs: Khufu, Khafre and Menkaure.

- The pyramids are a symbol of the sun god that the ancient Egyptians worshipped.

- The pyramids were meant to be a direct pathway to the heavens.

Q What were the names of the three pharaohs who built the three biggest pyramids?

Learning to build the pyramids

This is the final stage of pyramid building. It is Khufu's pyramid at Giza. You can see it is made of huge blocks of limestone. Further blocks once covered the surface to make it smooth.

Pyramids were built as burial places for pharaohs. The three Great Pyramids are the work of three pharaohs. They were built in a single century about 4,500 years ago. They were only built after a long period of experiments with other pyramids.

If we look at all of the pyramids in Egypt we can see how the idea of the Great Pyramid came about.

The first pyramid was made of simple steps using clay bricks. Later pyramids were covered in stone blocks to give them smooth sides.

There are over 100 pyramids just south of Cairo (formerly Memphis). The southern ones are the oldest. This is the first pyramid – the Step Pyramid of Djoser.

Did you know… ?

- The first pharaohs were buried in chambers in the rock below the pyramids.

- Later, the burial chambers were made within the pyramids. There were tiny shafts leading from the chambers to the outside world. These pointed directly at important stars.

This pyramid is bigger than the Step Pyramid. It was begun too steeply and, when it was in danger of collapse, the upper part was built at a shallower angle. That is why it is called the Bent Pyramid.

Q **Why was it dangerous to build pyramids with steep sides?**

The Sphinx

The Egyptians made sculptures of a creature that is part lion, part human. It is called a sphinx. The largest sphinx in the world is called The Sphinx, and it was sculpted out of solid rock close to the pyramids at Giza.

The Sphinx is one of the biggest sculptures in the world. It is 20 m tall and 57 m long. The head may originally have been carved as a likeness of King Khafre, whose pyramid is nearby.

The nose and the beard are now missing.

The Sphinx is wearing a traditional headdress. This is called a nemes headdress.

The Sphinx is in front of the pyramid built for Khafre.

Did you know... ?

- That sphinxes were creatures that protected the pharaoh.
- There are hundreds of sphinxes on the routes leading to ancient Egyptian temples as well as The Sphinx by the Great Pyramids.

Q How do you think the Sphinx might have looked with a beard? Look at page 25 and then make a drawing.

Temples by the Nile

There are many great temples beside the Nile. The biggest and most famous are near Luxor, once called Thebes, a capital of ancient Egypt.

An Egyptian temple was a building in which the pharaoh and his priests worshipped the gods. The ancient Egyptians believed that the temple for a god or goddess was their home. This meant that temples had to be the best buildings that the Egyptians could make.

The ancient Egyptian temple was a very complicated place, with many courtyards and halls. It was always approached by an avenue from the River Nile.

At Luxor, the avenue is lined by sphinxes. The gigantic sloping front wall is called a pylon. It is the entrance to the temple.

This picture looks along the avenue of sphinxes (1) to the gateway (pylon) (2) of the temple. Imagine the pharaoh approaching the temple. There would have been brightly coloured flags on poles beside the gateway. Carvings on the temple wall would have been painted, too. The sanctuary (4) was inside the temple behind the courtyard (3).

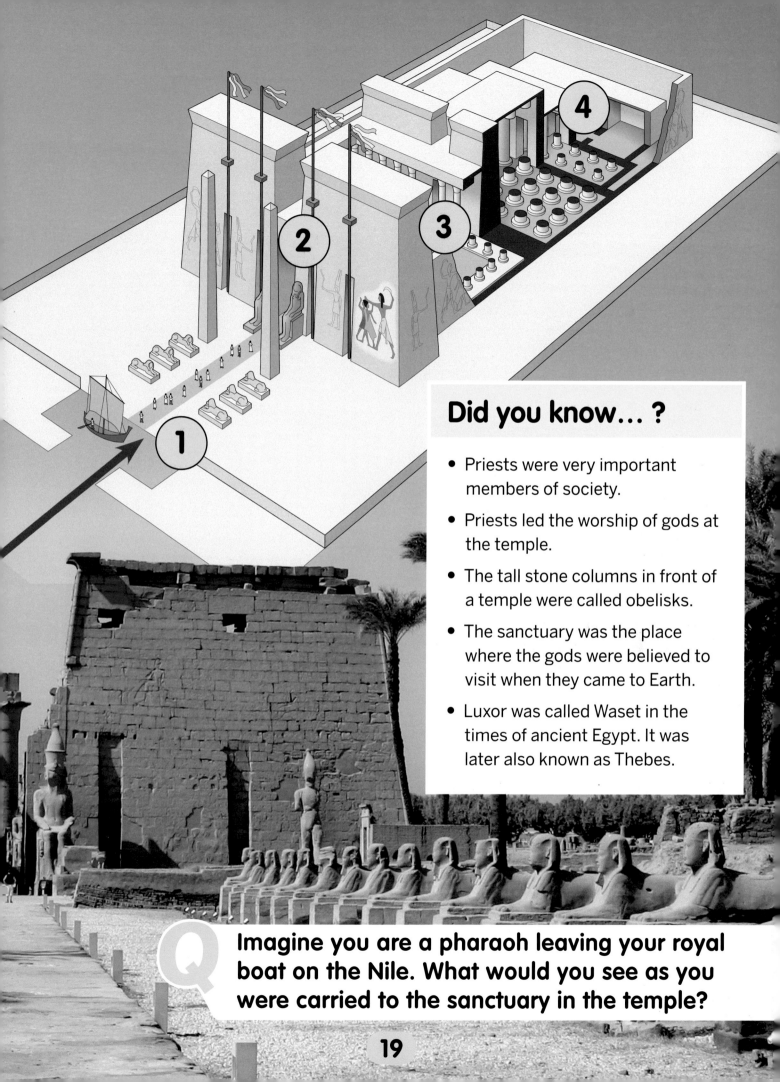

Did you know… ?

- Priests were very important members of society.

- Priests led the worship of gods at the temple.

- The tall stone columns in front of a temple were called obelisks.

- The sanctuary was the place where the gods were believed to visit when they came to Earth.

- Luxor was called Waset in the times of ancient Egypt. It was later also known as Thebes.

Q Imagine you are a pharaoh leaving your royal boat on the Nile. What would you see as you were carried to the sanctuary in the temple?

Temple of columns

The ancient Egyptian temples had many halls. However, the ancient Egyptians did not know how to build arches or domes and so all of their buildings have flat roofs made from heavy stone slabs. Large numbers of columns were needed to support them. In ancient Egyptian times the halls would have been very dark, mysterious places.

Did you know… ?

- A hall of many tall columns is called a hypostyle hall.

- The columns are carved with hieroglyphs telling stories of the gods and pharaohs.

- The columns were once richly painted and a little of the paint survives after 3,000 years.

- The ceilings of the halls were painted blue with white stars to symbolise the night sky and the heavens where the gods lived.

The columns are often shaped to represent **papyrus** stems. The column tops represent flowers in bud, open flowers and other decorative features. Look for the different patterns on the column tops.

Q Looking at the people in the photograph above, can you estimate the height of the columns?

21

Tutankhamun

Did you know... ?

- Tutankhamun means 'living image of the god Amun'.
- He was originally called Tutankhaten but he changed his name when he became king.
- Tutankhamun's tomb was found in the Valley of the Kings (on the opposite side of the River Nile to Luxor).

Egypt was ruled by kings, who we also call pharaohs. Tutankhamun ruled Egypt between 1334 and 1325 BC. Tutankhamun died when he was about 17, but no one is certain how he died. Some think it was from natural causes, such as an infection, some think he had a fatal accident, and some even think he was murdered.

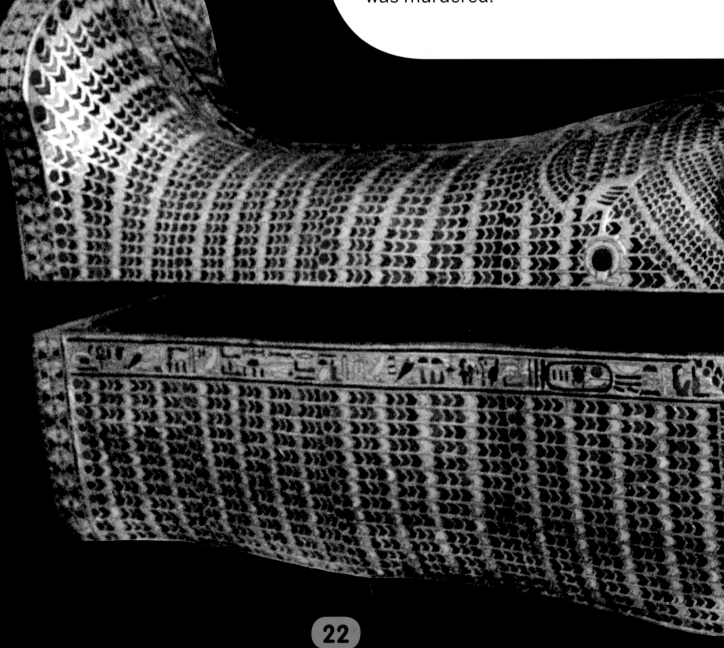

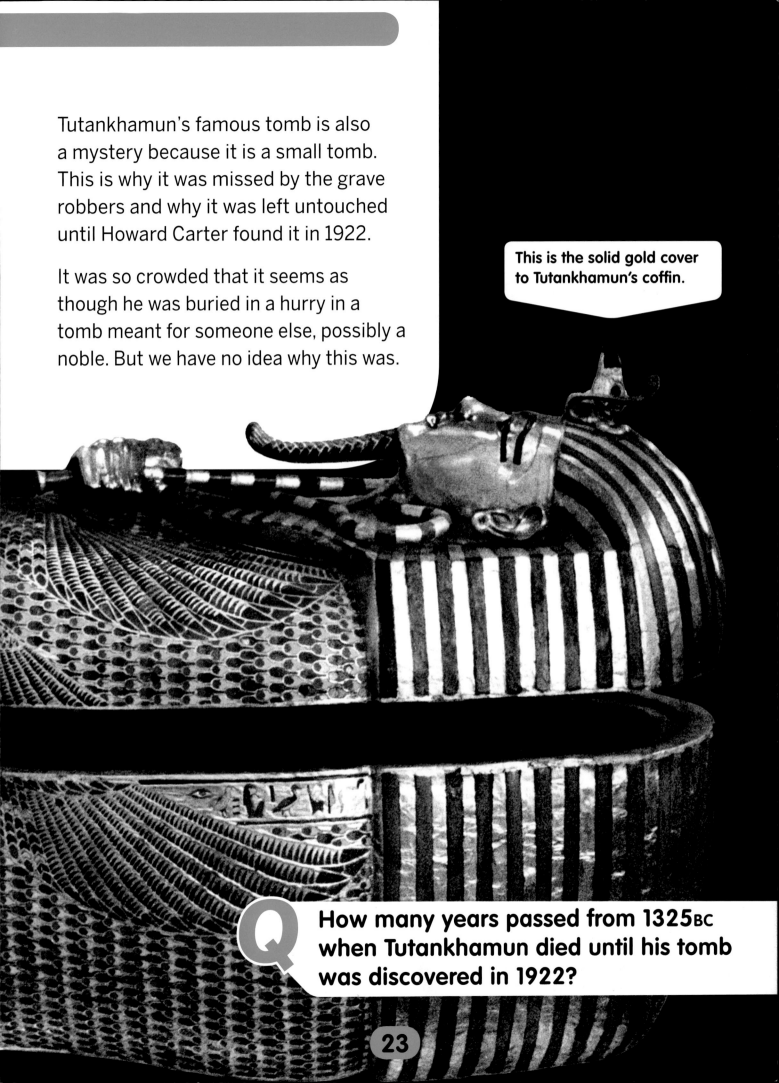

Tutankhamun's famous tomb is also a mystery because it is a small tomb. This is why it was missed by the grave robbers and why it was left untouched until Howard Carter found it in 1922.

It was so crowded that it seems as though he was buried in a hurry in a tomb meant for someone else, possibly a noble. But we have no idea why this was.

This is the solid gold cover to Tutankhamun's coffin.

Q How many years passed from 1325BC when Tutankhamun died until his tomb was discovered in 1922?

Ramesses the Great

Ramesses II ruled for 66 years from 1279 BC, when he was 30 years old, to 1213 BC, when he died aged 96.

In his long life, he had 200 wives, 96 sons and 60 daughters.

Ramesses undertook vast building projects. These always had **colossal** statues and pictures of himself. Even in his lifetime he was thought of as a god and called Ramesses the Great.

This is the temple at Abu Simbel showing four colossal statues of Ramesses.

Did you know… ?

- Most of the giant seated statues in front of ancient Egyptian temples are of Ramesses.

- Most of the battle scenes of Ramesses show him 'smiting' – that is, defeating – the Hittites (ancient Turks) at the battle of Kadesh.

Here you can see Ramesses (large) literally smashing an army of the neighbouring Hittites (small) and taking them into captivity.

Q Why was Ramesses II called 'The Great'?

Gods

The ancient Egyptians believed the sky, the earth and their land were connected, and that the gods lived in the sky and in the earth. They believed this was where people might go when they died.

The Egyptians worshipped many gods and told long and complex stories about them. The gods were often shown in sculptures and paintings as having the heads of animals.

The pharaoh was believed to be a link between the gods and the people. He was also believed to be a living god and be protected by a falcon-headed god called Horus. The living king was believed to be connected to the Sun god, Re, and the dead king was seen to be connected to Osiris, the god of the **underworld**. So kings built pyramids up towards Re and the stars, and chambers below the pyramids, to show they were connected to Osiris, too.

The god Re.

The god Horus.

26

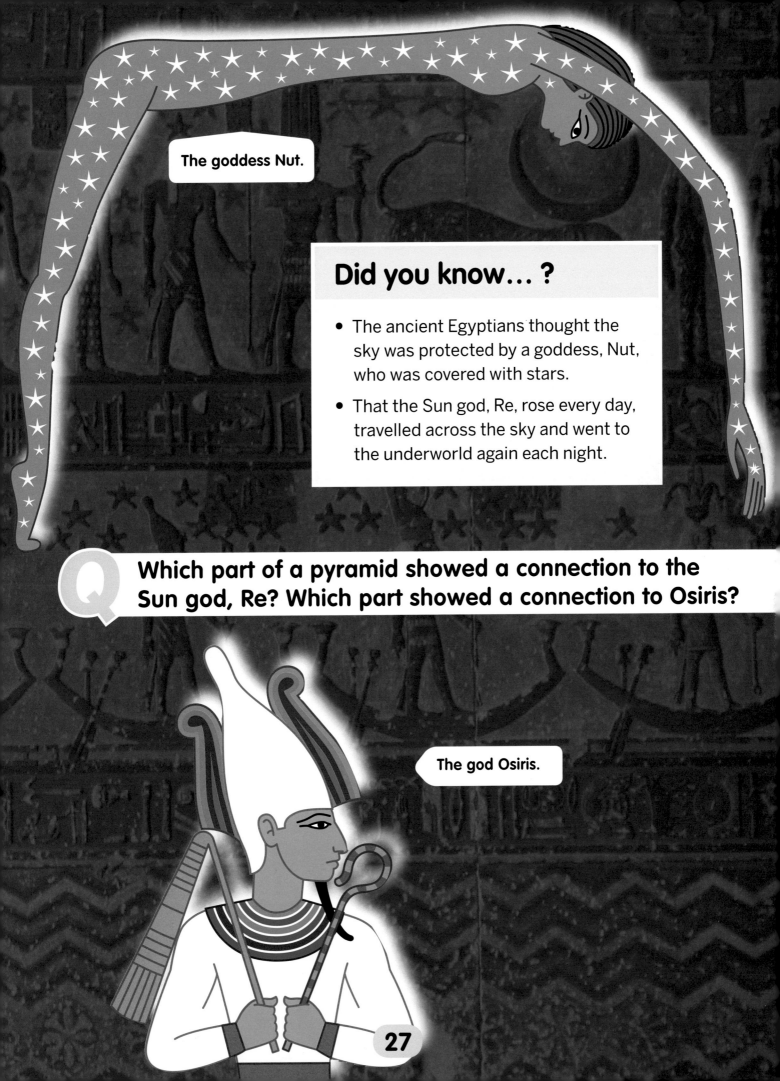

The goddess Nut.

Did you know… ?

- The ancient Egyptians thought the sky was protected by a goddess, Nut, who was covered with stars.
- That the Sun god, Re, rose every day, travelled across the sky and went to the underworld again each night.

Q Which part of a pyramid showed a connection to the Sun god, Re? Which part showed a connection to Osiris?

The god Osiris.

Mummification

When people are buried in the dry, salty sands of the desert, their bodies do not rot away, but instead dry out and are preserved. This is a kind of natural mummification. But when the ancient Egyptians began burying their dead in coffins to protect them from wild animals, the bodies started to decay. So the ancient Egyptians had to find a way of copying natural mummification.

Since mummification was a long and very expensive process only pharaohs and the most important nobles were mummified and placed in tombs.

The pharaohs and nobles were then buried with many treasures and furniture – even food and slaves (shabti figures) so that they could continue to live in luxury with the gods.

The mummified body was placed in one or more wooden coffins, and the coffins were put in a stone box (sarcophagus).

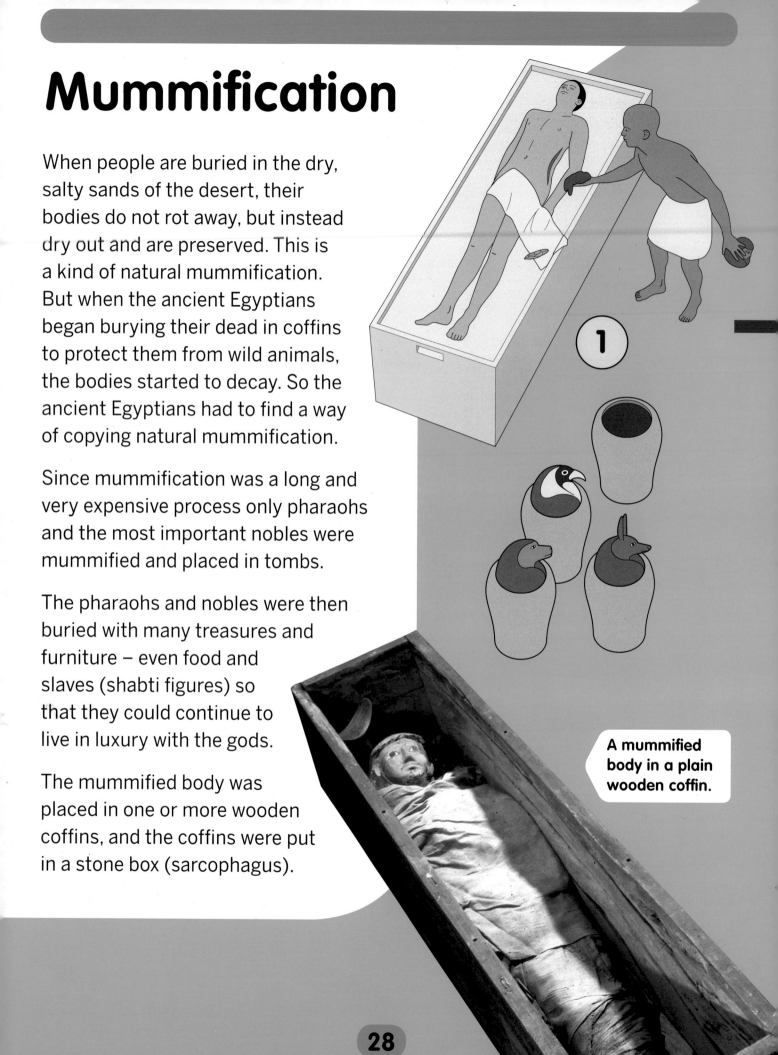

A mummified body in a plain wooden coffin.

The stages of mummification: (1) The entrails are removed and placed in canopic jars; (2) The body is dried out with salt; (3) The skin has oils rubbed into it; (4) The body is wrapped in bandages with good luck charms; (5) The body is placed in a coffin.

Did you know...?

- The earliest surviving Egyptian mummies date from around 3300 BC.

- The embalmers who mummified pharaohs and nobles took seventy days.

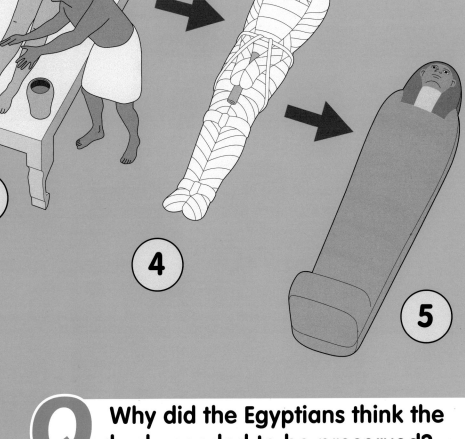

Q **Why did the Egyptians think the body needed to be preserved?**

Try these...

An Egyptian costume

Make a costume from the items shown in these pictures:

An Egyptian boy

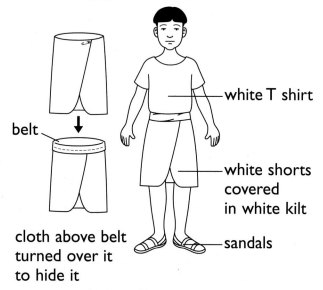

belt

cloth above belt turned over it to hide it

white T shirt

white shorts covered in white kilt

sandals

An Egyptian girl

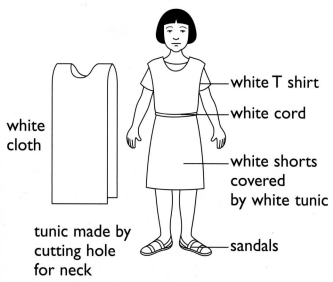

white cloth

tunic made by cutting hole for neck

white T shirt

white cord

white shorts covered by white tunic

sandals

Measure the Egyptian way

The Egyptians used the following units for measuring:

The digit	=	The width of a finger.
The palm	=	Four digits.
The hand	=	Five digits.
The cubit	=	28 digits (the distance from fingertip to elbow).

The fathom = Four cubits (height from the ground to the top of a person's hairline on the forehead).

- Measure out some distances in centimetres and then in the Egyptian way. You could try the width and height of this open book, the height of a coffee mug, the width of a chair, and the height of a friend. Which way of measuring is easier?

Egyptian writing

As well as writing in hieroglyphs, the Egyptians used a simple script to write on papyrus. This can be partly matched to our alphabet.

Write a message in the script and ask a friend to translate it. Challenge your friend to write a message for you to translate.

Use Egyptian numbers

The Egyptians used seven signs for numbers:

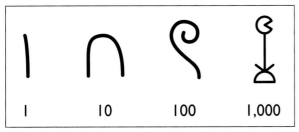

I	10	100	1,000

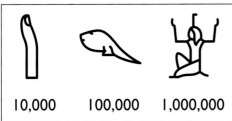

10,000	100,000	1,000,000

- The sign for the larger number is always written in front of the sign for the smaller number. For example, ∩ I I is the way to write 12.

- Write down your age and the ages of people in your family. If you have made measurements in the Egyptian way write the numbers in the Egyptian way, too.

A	B	C	D	E	F	G	H	I

J	K	L	M	N	O	P	Q

R	S	T	U	V	W	Y	Z

Measuring time with a water clock

The Egyptians used a water clock to measure time.

Diagram 1

Diagram 2

- Ask an adult to cut a plastic bottle into a top half and a bottom half.

- Flatten a piece of Plasticine and make a small hole in its centre, as diagram 1 shows.

- Press the Plasticine across the top of the bottle.

- Turn the top half of the bottle upside down and put it in the bottom half, as diagram 2 shows.

- Make a scale and stick it on the side.

- Put water in the bottle top and let it drip through.

- Mark the water level in the bottom part every minute.

- Use your water clock to measure time periods, such as two minutes and four minutes.

- Compare the time measured with a watch or clock. How accurate is the water clock?

Glossary

canopic A word used to describe a jar which holds the entrails of a person.

colossal Huge or enormous.

Djoser One of the earliest Egyptian kings. Reign: 2687–2668 bc. He was buried in the Step Pyramid.

entrails The organs from inside a person's body, such as the stomach and intestines.

hieroglyph A picture of an object which stands for a letter or a word.

irrigate To supply water to an area of land using channels.

Khafre (or Chephren) A king of the Old Kingdom. Reign: 2558–2532 bc. He was buried in the middle Great Pyramid at Giza (Cairo).

Khufu (or Cheops) A king of the Old Kingdom. Reign: 2589–2566 bc. He was buried in the tallest of the pyramids at Giza (Cairo).

Menkaure A king of the Old Kingdom. Reign: 2532–2503 bc. He was buried in the smaller of the three Great Pyramids at Giza (Cairo).

nemes headdress A piece of cloth tied around the head to protect the wearer from the Sun.

papyrus A tall plant that grows on flooded land and can be used to make a kind of paper on which the Egyptians wrote.

tomb A place where dead people are buried.

underworld A place under the ground where the ancient Egyptians believed dead people continued to exist.

Index

Curriculum Visions

Curriculum Visions Explorers
This series provides straightforward introductions to key worlds and ideas.

You might also be interested in
Our slightly more detailed book, 'The ancient Egyptians 2nd Edition'. There is a Teacher's Guide to match 'The ancient Egyptians 2nd Edition'. Additional notes in PDF format are also available from the publisher to support 'Exploring ancient Egypt 2nd Edition'. All of these products are suitable for KS2.

There's much more online including videos
You will find multimedia resources covering the ancient Egyptians as well as other periods of history, geography, religion, MFL, maths, music, spelling and more at:

www.CurriculumVisions.com

(Subscription required)

A CVP Book
This second edition © Atlantic Europe Publishing 2013

First edition 2007. First reprint 2008.

The right of Brian Knapp to be identified as the author of this work has been asserted by him in accordance with the Copyright, Designs and Patents Act 1988.

All rights reserved. No part of this publication may be reproduced, stored in a retrieval system, or transmitted in any form or by any means, electronic, mechanical, photocopying, recording or otherwise, without prior permission of the copyright holder.

Author
Brian Knapp, BSc, PhD

Consulting Editor and Contributor
Peter Riley, BSc, C Biol, MI Biol, PGCE
(material on pages 30–31 is based on the Curriculum Visions' The ancient Egyptians Teacher's Guide authored by Peter Riley)

Educational Consultant
JM Smith (former Deputy Head of Wellfield School, Burnley, Lancashire); the Librarians of Hertfordshire School Library Service

Senior Designer
Adele Humphries, BA, PGCE

Editor
Gillian Gatehouse

Illustrations
David Woodroffe except p1, 4–5 Mark Stacey

Designed and produced by
Atlantic Europe Publishing

Printed in China by
WKT Company Ltd

Exploring ancient Egypt 2nd Edition – Curriculum Visions
A CIP record for this book is available from the British Library.

Paperback ISBN 978 1 86214 779 9

Picture credits
All photographs are from the Earthscape Picture Library, except the following: (c=centre t=top b=bottom l=left r=right bygonetimes/Alamy p22–23; The Granger Collection, New York p28.

This product is manufactured from sustainable managed forests. For every tree cut down at least one more is planted.